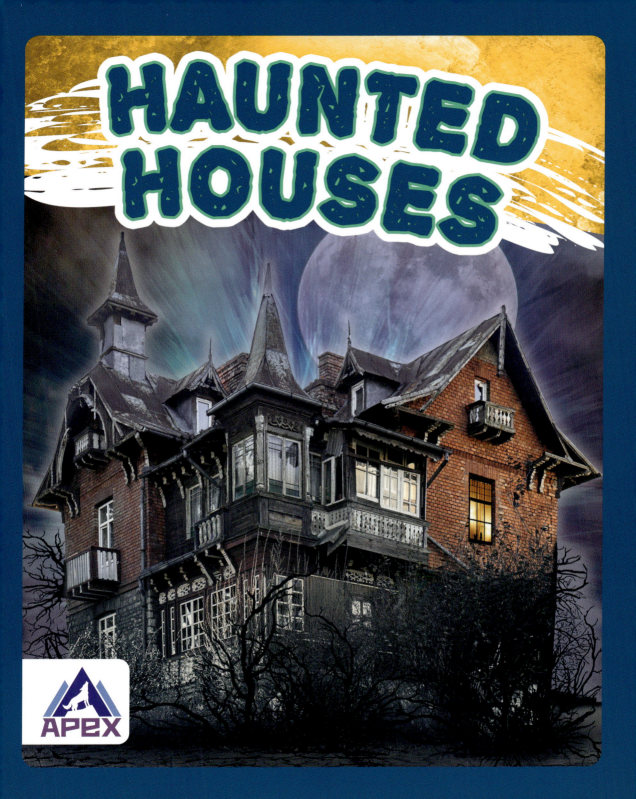

HAUNTED HOUSES

BY MEG GAERTNER

WWW.APEXEDITIONS.COM

Copyright © 2022 by Apex Editions, Mendota Heights, MN 55120. All rights reserved. No part of this book may be reproduced or utilized in any form or by any means without written permission from the publisher.

Apex is distributed by North Star Editions:
sales@northstareditions.com | 888-417-0195

Produced for Apex by Red Line Editorial.

Photographs ©: Shutterstock Images, cover (house), 1 (house), 4–5, 6–7, 8, 9, 10–11, 12, 13, 14–15, 16–17, 18, 20–21, 22–23, 24–25, 26–27, 29; Unsplash, cover (background), 1 (background); iStockphoto, 19

Library of Congress Control Number: 2021915674

ISBN
978-1-63738-163-2 (hardcover)
978-1-63738-199-1 (paperback)
978-1-63738-268-4 (ebook pdf)
978-1-63738-235-6 (hosted ebook)

Printed in the United States of America
Mankato, MN
012022

NOTE TO PARENTS AND EDUCATORS

Apex books are designed to build literacy skills in striving readers. Exciting, high-interest content attracts and holds readers' attention. The text is carefully leveled to allow students to achieve success quickly. Additional features, such as bolded glossary words for difficult terms, help build comprehension.

TABLE OF CONTENTS

CHAPTER 1
ENTER IF YOU DARE 5

CHAPTER 2
COMMON HAUNTINGS 11

CHAPTER 3
HAUNTED HISTORY 17

CHAPTER 4
SOME EXPLANATIONS 23

Comprehension Questions • 28

Glossary • 30

To Learn More • 31

About the Author • 31

Index • 32

CHAPTER 1
ENTER IF YOU DARE

The house sits alone on a hill. It is very old. The dark windows are like eyes. The open door is a mouth. Two friends dare to go inside.

Many haunted houses are in dark or lonely places.

The inside of a haunted house is often broken and dusty.

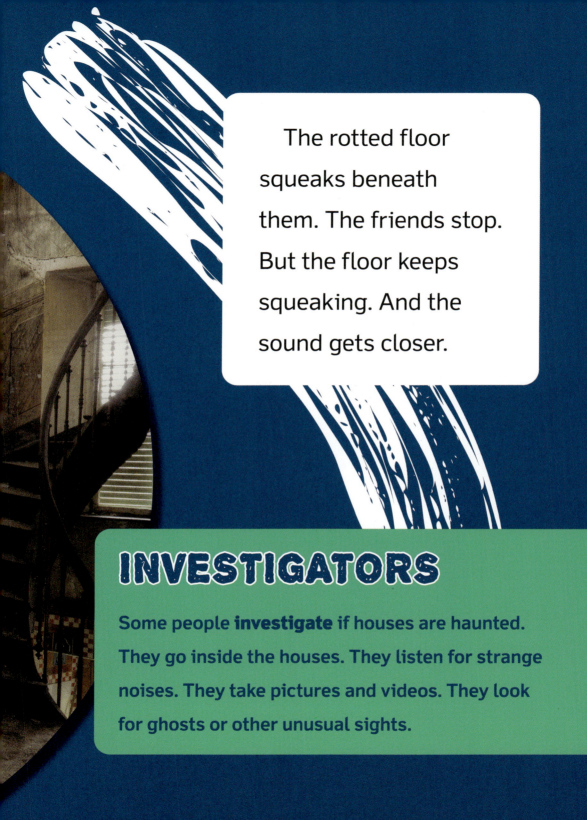

The rotted floor squeaks beneath them. The friends stop. But the floor keeps squeaking. And the sound gets closer.

INVESTIGATORS

Some people **investigate** if houses are haunted. They go inside the houses. They listen for strange noises. They take pictures and videos. They look for ghosts or other unusual sights.

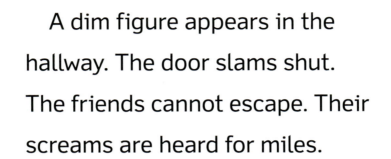

A dim figure appears in the hallway. The door slams shut. The friends cannot escape. Their screams are heard for miles.

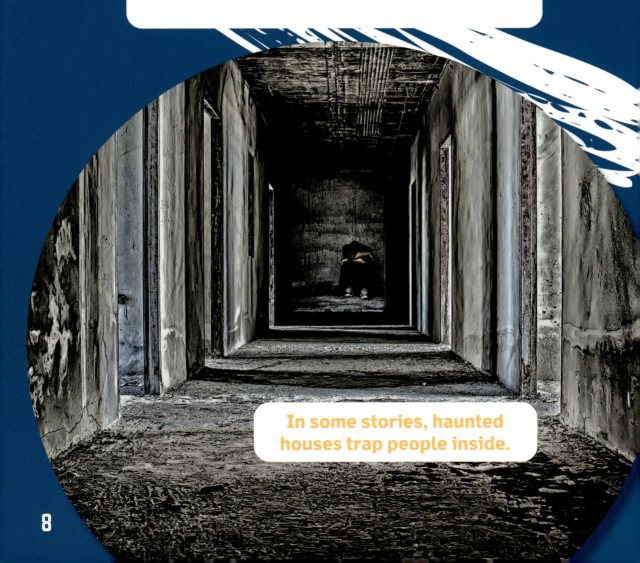

In some stories, haunted houses trap people inside.

The Winchester Mystery House is in California. It has doors and stairs that lead nowhere.

Haunted houses often have secret rooms. The strange floor plan makes people feel trapped.

CHAPTER 2
COMMON HAUNTINGS

Strange events happen in haunted houses. Some people blame spirits of the dead. The spirits are **restless**. They cause trouble.

Some spirits that haunt houses are visible. Others make sounds or move objects.

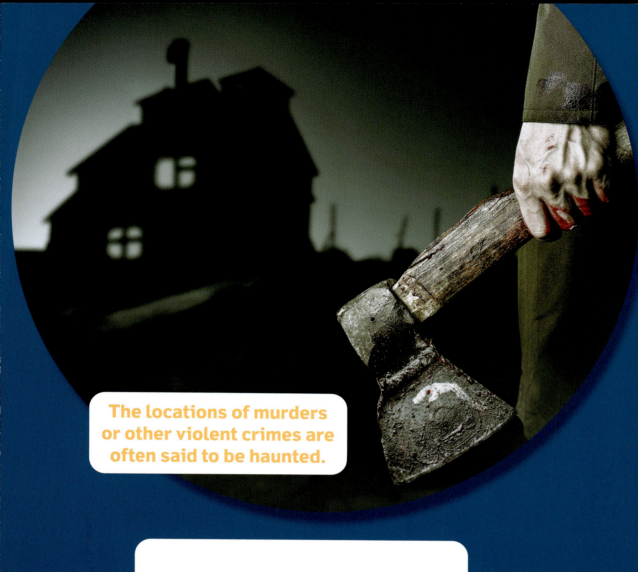

The locations of murders or other violent crimes are often said to be haunted.

Haunted houses often have troubled pasts. Past **residents** may have died or gone missing.

HAUNTED HOTEL

Jails, hotels, and other buildings with troubled pasts can be haunted. In one haunted hotel, lights turn on and off. Objects move. Guests suddenly feel cold. They hear children laughing.

People report seeing ghosts in many parts of the Stanley Hotel in Estes Park, Colorado.

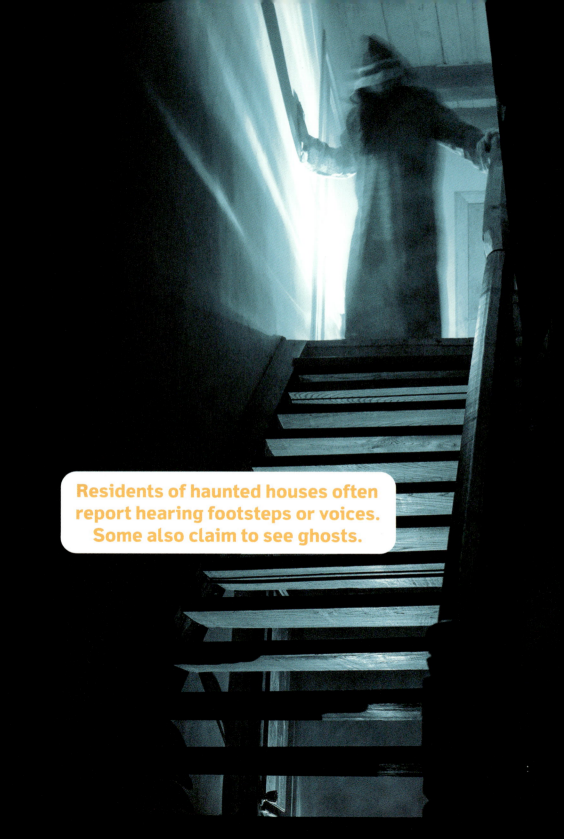

Residents of haunted houses often report hearing footsteps or voices. Some also claim to see ghosts.

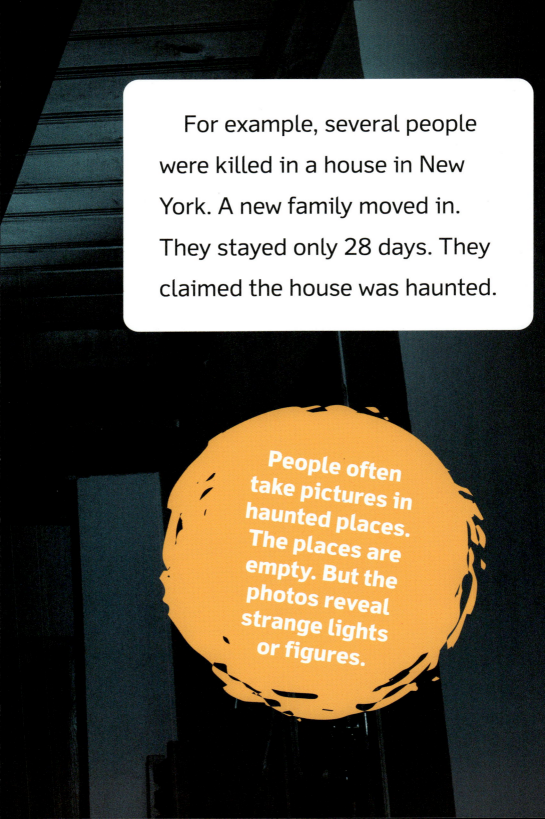

For example, several people were killed in a house in New York. A new family moved in. They stayed only 28 days. They claimed the house was haunted.

People often take pictures in haunted places. The places are empty. But the photos reveal strange lights or figures.

CHAPTER 3

HAUNTED HISTORY

The earliest story of a haunted house comes from ancient Rome. People said they heard chains rattling. The spirit of an old man appeared.

In stories, ghosts often slam or rattle doors. They may also tap on windows or walls.

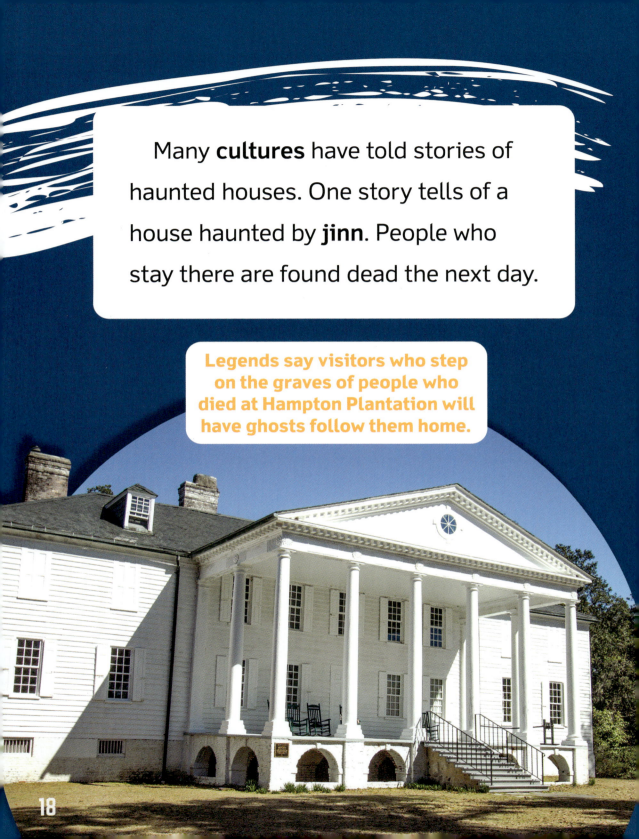

Many **cultures** have told stories of haunted houses. One story tells of a house haunted by **jinn**. People who stay there are found dead the next day.

Legends say visitors who step on the graves of people who died at Hampton Plantation will have ghosts follow them home.

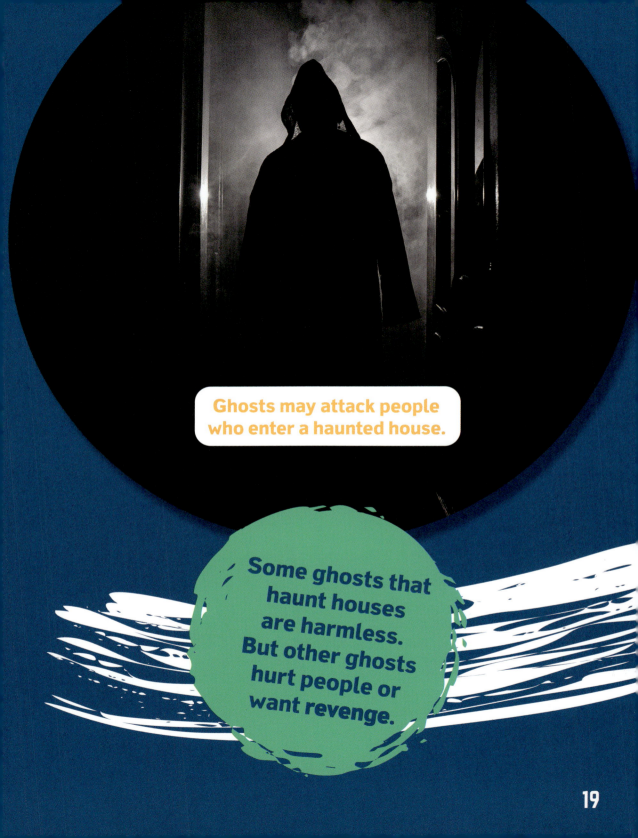

Ghosts may attack people who enter a haunted house.

Some ghosts that haunt houses are harmless. But other ghosts hurt people or want revenge.

Haunted house attractions are often built to look like old mansions or castles.

Haunted house **attractions** have become popular, too. Visitors go inside them for a fun scare.

GETTING THE CHILLS

In Japan, people visit haunted houses in summer. Some Japanese people believe August is when family spirits return. Also, the weather is hot then. Scared people often **shiver**. This can help them cool down.

CHAPTER 4
SOME EXPLANATIONS

People often hear strange sounds in haunted houses. Walls rattle. Stairs squeak. But all houses tend to make noise.

Many haunted houses are old and falling apart.

Plus, the heating in old houses sometimes breaks. It can give off a poisonous gas. People who breathe this gas may feel weak or hear things.

Another reason is the power of **suggestion**. People enter a haunted house feeling afraid. That feeling shapes how they explain what happens.

EXPECTATIONS

Expectations shape what people think, do, and feel. People expect scary things to happen in a haunted house. So, if wind pushes a door shut, people may blame a ghost.

COMPREHENSION QUESTIONS

Write your answers on a separate piece of paper.

1. Write a sentence describing the main ideas of Chapter 4.

2. Would you want to visit a haunted house? Why or why not?

3. Where did the first haunted house story come from?

   A. New York
   B. Japan
   C. Rome

4. A friend tells you a new movie is really bad. According to the power of suggestion, what might you do when you see the movie?

   A. You might notice only bad things about the movie.
   B. You might really enjoy the movie.
   C. You might forget what happens in the movie.

5. What does **harmless** mean in this book?

*Some ghosts that haunt houses are **harmless**. But other ghosts hurt people or want revenge.*

    A. wanting revenge
    B. not doing anything
    C. not causing problems

6. What does **rattle** mean in this book?

*People often hear strange sounds in haunted houses. Walls **rattle**. Stairs squeak.*

    A. to stay very quiet
    B. to make noise by shaking
    C. to fill with water

Answer key on page 32.

GLOSSARY

attractions
Places people go to for fun.

cultures
Groups of people and the ways they live, including their beliefs and laws.

expectations
Ideas about what something will be like.

investigate
To try to find out the truth about something.

jinn
Powerful spirits in some Arabic stories.

residents
People who live in a certain place.

restless
Unable to rest.

revenge
Getting back at someone who has caused hurt or anger.

shiver
To shake as a result of feeling scared or cold.

suggestion
When people's thoughts, feelings, or actions are shaped by an idea they have or are given.

TO LEARN MORE

BOOKS

Bingham, Jane. *Ghosts and Haunted Houses: Myth or Reality?* North Mankato, MN: Capstone Press, 2019.

Owings, Lisa. *Haunted Houses*. Minneapolis: Bellwether Media, 2019.

Ransom, Candice. *Eerie Haunted Houses*. Minneapolis: Lerner Publications, 2020.

ONLINE RESOURCES

Visit **www.apexeditions.com** to find links and resources related to this title.

ABOUT THE AUTHOR

Meg Gaertner is a children's book editor and writer. She lives in Minneapolis, where she enjoys swing dancing and spending time outside.

INDEX

D
doors, 5, 8, 27

E
expectations, 27

F
feelings, 9, 13, 24–25, 27

G
ghosts, 7, 19, 27

H
hearing, 13, 17, 23–25

J
Japan, 21
jinn, 18

L
lights, 13, 15

N
New York, 15

P
pictures, 7, 15
poisonous gas, 24

R
Rome, 17

S
sounds, 7, 23, 25
spirits, 11, 17, 21
suggestion, 27

V
videos, 7

W
walls, 23
windows, 5

Answer Key:
1. Answers will vary; **2.** Answers will vary; **3.** C; **4.** A; **5.** C; **6.** B